CONSUMER MATHEMAT
TRANSPORTATION

W9-AXP-849

CONTENTS

Author: **Thomas W. Hazard, Ph.D.**

Editor-in-Chief: **Richard W. Wheeler, M.A.Ed.**

Editor: **Stephany L. Sykes**

Consulting Editor: **Robert L. Zenor, M.A., M.S.**

Illustrator: **Thomas R. Rush**

Alpha Omega Publications®

804 N. 2nd Ave. E., Rock Rapids, IA 51246-1759

TRANSPORTATION

Americans are the most travel-oriented people in the world. When all the means of transportation are lumped together—cars, trucks, trains, planes, barges, highways, railways, and canals, the investment in transportation amounts to over $500 billion. This investment is about $2,000 for every man, woman, and child in this country.

We are so dependent upon the vast transportation network that spans our continent, that if this network were to cease suddenly, our economy would grind to a virtual halt. Essential goods depend on transportation to get to consumers, and workers depend on transportation to get them to their jobs. The transportation industry employs over 5 million workers in this country. Over 110 million automobiles are owned by people in the United States. These figures should give you some idea of the relative importance of transportation to our lives.

In this LIFEPAC you will learn how transportation affects the consumer in terms of costs and benefits. You will be given examples of how to figure the costs of owning and operating an automobile, how to compare insurance rates, and how to figure the relative efficiency of certain kinds of transportation. You will also learn some useful tips for traveling abroad, including how to exchange foreign currency, how to estimate travel costs, and how to figure duties one must pay on articles brought back to the United States.

OBJECTIVES

Read these objectives. The objectives tell you what you will be able to do when you have successfully completed this LIFEPAC.

When you have finished this LIFEPAC, you should be able

1. To compute the cost of financing an automobile;

2. To compute operating costs of an automobile;

3. To make comparisons among types of automobile insurance coverage;

4. To work time, distance, and rate problems;

5. To adjust time based on time zones;

6. To calculate currency-exchange rates; and

7. To make cost-benefit comparisons with regard to travel.

Survey the LIFEPAC. Ask yourself some questions about this study. Write your questions here.

_____

_____

_____

_____

_____

_____

_____

I. FINANCING AND OPERATING AN AUTOMOBILE

OBJECTIVES

1. To compute the cost of financing an automobile.
2. To compute operating costs of an automobile.
3. To make comparisons among types of automobile insurance coverage.

Few automobile drivers understand the actual costs of owning and operating their cars. Most people think that the cost of an automobile is the sticker price displayed on the car window as it sits in the showroom or on the dealer lot. However, since very few people pay cash for a car, they often pay twice as much money for the car because of the interest charges on the financing contract.

Financing and operating a car are just part of the economics picture. Operating your car includes much more than putting in gas and occasionally a quart of oil. Maintenance costs including repairs and parts, _depreciation_, and insurance add up to significant cash outlays over the period of ownership.

When a person buys an automobile, he must pay an interest charge along with the price of the car. The buyer can pay a sum of money, called a *down payment*, before the total cost of the car is figured to lower the interest amount and total cost of the car. This section explains how to figure the true annual interest rate and other figures related to buying a car.

PROCEDURE

To determine the rate of interest charged to finance an automobile, complete these steps: (1) Find the product of twice the number of payments in one year (y) and the amount of interest charged over the full contract period (c) and (2) divide the resultant from Step 1. by the product of the unpaid balance (cash price - down payment) (m) and the number of payments to be made over the contract period plus 1 ($n + 1$).

$I = \dfrac{2yc}{m(n + 1)}$, where I is the true annual interest rate, y is the number of payments in one year, c is the amount of interest charges, m is the amount of unpaid balance, and n is the number of payments made.

Model 1: You wish to buy a new Toyota. The dealer tells you the price is $5,050 complete, with license and taxes included. You want to put down $500 in down payment. You agree to finance the balance through a finance company that quotes your payments over four years as $165 per month. What is the true annual interest rate?

c = (amount of monthy payments)(number of months) - unpaid balance
= (monthly payment)(n) - m
= $165 x 48 - ($5,050 - $500)
= $7,920 - $4,550 = $3,370

$I = \dfrac{2(12)(3,370)}{4,550(48 + 1)}$

$= \dfrac{80,880}{222,950} = 36\%$

Model 2: You are financing the payment for a used car. The dealer says he will sell you the car for $2,995 after a $295 down payment. He also says you can finance the balance at an 8½% true annual interest rate and that your payments will be $85.50 per month for 36 months. Is the dealer correct in quoting 8½% as the interest rate?

$$c = \$85.50 \times 36 - (\$2,995 - \$295)$$
$$= \$3,078 - \$2,700 = \$378$$

$$I = \frac{2(12)(378)}{2,700(36 + 1)}$$
$$= \frac{9,072}{99,900} = 9.1\%$$

The answer is no, since 9.1% is greater than 8½%.

Model 3: Purchase price of car is $2,500. No down payment. The contract calls for a 10% true annual interest rate and monthly payments over a 24-month period. What is the amount of monthly payment?

$$10\% = \frac{2(12)c}{2,500(24 + 1)}$$
$$24c = (0.10)(2,500)(25)$$
$$24c = 6,250$$
$$c = \$260.42$$

Since the amount of monthly payment equals the balance of payments plus interest charges divided by the total number of payments, the amount of monthly payment

$$= \frac{2,500 + 260.42}{24} = \$115.02.$$

Compute the following interest-rate problems.

1.1 Purchase price of car = $4,250
Amount of down payment = $700
Number of payments made in year = 12
Number of payments made over contract period = 24
Amount of monthly payment = $178.25
True annual interest rate?

1.2   Purchase price of car = $6,650
        Amount of trade-in value = $2,000
        Number of payments made in year = 12
        Number of payments made = 36
        Amount of monthly payment = $198.75
        True annual interest rate?

        _____

1.3   Purchase price of car = $3,875
        Amount of down payment = $385
        Number of payments made in year = 12
        Number of payments made = 30
        True annual interest rate = 12%
        Amount of monthly payment?

        _____

1.4   Purchase price of car = $5,200
        Amount of down payment = $550
        Number of payments made in year = 12
        Number of payments made = 42
        True annual interest rate = 20%
        Amount of monthly payment?

        _____

1.5   You price a new car. The cost is $6,995. Your
        credit union quotes you a 9% true annual interest
        rate for financing. You wish to pay off the loan
        in 48 payments and want to keep the car payment
        at $155 per month. How large a down payment must
        you make to meet these conditions?
        (Hint: Since c = $155 x 48 - m, substitute this
        expression for c into the true annual interest
        rate formula and solve the problem accordingly.)

        _____

1.6   True annual interest rate = 18.5%
        Interest charges = $681.51
        Number of monthly payments = 30
        Total amount financed?

        _____

5

Automobile operating costs include such things as gas; oil; repairs; parts; maintenance; depreciation; insurance; and taxes, both Federal and state. We shall assume that the price of gas and oil includes taxes.

PROCEDURE

To calculate gas and oil charges as a cost per mile driven, divide the amount spent on gas and oil by the number of miles driven.

Model 1: Your total gas and oil charges for the year amount to $1,080. You estimate that you drove 14,000 miles during the year. What is the cost in cents per mile for gas and oil?

$$\text{Cost} = \frac{\$1,080}{14,000} = 0.077, \text{ or } 7.7\text{¢ per mile}$$

Model 2: Your automobile gets about 16 miles to the gallon. You drive 16,000 miles. If the cost at the pump is $1.10 per gallon, and you also paid for 10 quarts of oil at $1.75 per quart, what is the cost of gas and oil per mile?

$$\text{Gallons purchased} = \frac{16,000}{16} = 1,000$$

Cost of gas = 1,000 x 1.10 = $1100.00
Cost of oil = 10 x $1.75 = $17.50
Total cost of gas and oil = $1100.00 + $17.50 = 1117.50

$$\text{Cost of gas and oil} = \frac{\$1117.50}{16,000} = 0.07 \text{ or } 7\text{¢ per mile.}$$

PROCEDURE

To determine the cost per mile for repairs, parts, and maintenance, divide the total cost of these items by the number of miles driven.

Model 1: You determine that you paid $48.50 for parts, $250 in repair bills not covered by insurance, and $178 in service costs during the past year. Your odometer shows that you drove the car 15,000 miles during the year. What is the cost per mile for these operating costs?

Parts = $ 48.50
Repairs =   250.00
Servicing   178.00
(maintenance)=
Total = $476.50

Operating costs = $\frac{\$476.50}{15,000}$ = 0.0318, or 3.2¢ per mile.

Model 2: Repairs = $480
Parts = $275
Maintenance = $360
Miles driven = 18,500
Operating costs?

Total cost of operating
costs listed = $480 + $275 + $360
= $1,115
Operating costs = $\frac{\$1,115}{18,500}$ = 0.06, or 6¢ per mile.

DEFINITION

Depreciation is a lessening, or lowering, in value of an asset based upon its age.

Now that we know what depreciation is, we shall learn how to determine its cost relative to the automobile. The loss in value is the difference in the original value of the automobile and the resale or salvage value at the time the automobile is traded or scrapped.

PROCEDURE

To determine the cost of depreciation per mile driven:
(1) Subtract the estimated trade-in or salvage value from
the original cost of the automobile; (2) divide the
resulting loss in value by the number of years of use to
get the average yearly depreciation; and (3) divide the
average yearly depreciation by the average number of miles
driven to obtain the depreciation cost per mile driven.

Model 1: You purchased a car five years ago for
$3,400. You trade it in for $350 on a
new car. If you averaged 20,000 miles of
driving per year, what was the cost of
depreciation per mile driven?

Total depreciation = $3,400 - $350 = $3,050

Average yearly depreciation = $\frac{\$3,050}{5}$ = $610

Cost of depreciation = $\frac{\$610}{20,000}$ = 0.03, or 3¢ per mile.

Model 2: You drive a Mercury for 8 years and sell
it for $50 to a salvage company. It
originally cost you $2,450 new. The
odometer registered 92,000 miles when
you scrapped the car. What was the cost
of depreciation per mile driven?

Total depreciation = $2,450 - $50 = $2,400

Cost of depreciation = $\frac{\$2,400}{92,000}$ = 0.026, or 2.6¢ per
mile.

▬▬▬   Work the following automobile-operating costs
problems.

1.7   Gas and oil costs = $1,200
Miles driven = 12,500
Cost per mile?

_____

1.8   Gas and oil costs = $1,024
Cost per mile = 8¢
Miles driven?

_____

8

1.9   Gas mileage = 15.5 miles per gallon
       Miles driven = 14,500
       Price of gasoline = 66.9¢ per gallon
       Cost of oil used = $8.75
       Cost per mile for gas and oil?

       _____

1.10   Cost of repairs = $225
       Cost of parts = $165
       Cost of maintenance = $312
       Miles driven = 17,500
       Cost per mile?

       _____

1.11   Cost of repairs = $55
       Cost of parts = $3.50
       Average cost of maintenance = $8.50 per month
       Miles driven = 13,000
       Cost per mile?

       _____

1.12   Cost of repairs = $0
       Cost of parts = $165
       Cost of maintenance = $155
       Cost per mile = 3.2¢
       Miles driven?

       _____

1.13   Purchase price = $5,750
       Market value at resale = $3,250
       Years driven = 4
       Average number of miles driven per year = 16,025
       Cost of depreciation per mile?

       _____

1.14   Purchase price of automobile = $3,850
       Salvage value = $150
       Years driven = 9
       Average number of miles driven per year = 18,000
       Cost of depreciation per mile driven?

       _____

1.15　　Purchase price of automobile = $6,600
　　　　Resale value = $3,900
　　　　Years driven = 3
　　　　Cost of depreciation per mile driven = 9¢
　　　　Average number of miles driven per year?

_____

1.16　　Purchase price of automobile = $7,885
　　　　Years driven = 5
　　　　Cost of depreciation per mile driven = 8.5¢
　　　　Average number of miles driven per year = 15,000
　　　　Resale value?

_____

(Hint: First find the average depreciation per year
by multiplying the average miles driven by the cost
of depreciation per mile driven. Then substitute
the resulting figure into the formula for computing
depreciation per year to find the resale value.)

INSURANCE COST COMPARISONS

Insurance rates are high, to be sure.
This cost is partly because of the high
number of car accidents. Statistics show
that almost every driver in this
country will have been in an automobile
accident within ten years of driving.

Other reasons for rising insurance
rates are higher costs of repairs and
medical services due to inflation, larger
judgments awarded by courts in settling
liability suits, and legal fees and over-
head costs that amount to 56 cents out of
every $1 paid for insurance.

Buying appropriate coverage is not
an easy task. The different types of
coverage that are offered, the discounts
that are given to certain categories of
drivers, and the varying state requirements
all tend to confuse the average automobile
owner in his search for adequate protection.

The careful and patient automobile owner, however, can cut down on the cost of insurance by shopping around and comparing the premiums charged by different companies. Premiums for the same coverage can vary as much as 285%. Even though such a variance is an extreme case, the figure cited is officially documented by the Illinois State Department of Insurance.

The reason for so many forms of coverage is the nature of the automobile. An automobile can cause a variety of risks to its owner. It can be a source of liability for the owner and the operator; it may be damaged or destroyed by act of malice, or stolen, and it can cause the driver or his passenger to be killed or injured.

Let us examine the basic types of insurance coverage offered.

Two types of liability insurance are provided and, in many states, are compulsory. The first liability insurance is bodily injury coverage.

DEFINITION

Bodily injury insurance offers protection covering injury to other passengers during an accident involving the policy holder's vehicle. Minimum coverage is $10,000 for one person, with a maximum of $20,000 paid out if more than one person is injured.

Another form of liability insurance is property damage coverage.

DEFINITION

Property damage insurance offers protection against losses incurred to property belonging to persons other than the policy holder. The usual amount of coverage is $5,000.

Most policies combine liability coverage in a form of shorthand: for example, 10/20/5. The 10 stands for a $10,000 maximum that the insurance company will pay for injuries suffered by any one person. The 20 stands for a maximum of $20,000 that the insurance company will pay if more than one person is injured. The 5 represents a maximum of $5,000 that the insurance company will pay for damages to another car or to valuable property.

We indicated previously that 10/20/5 was the minimum coverage for liability insurance. Because of the reasons cited earlier, a policy holder is wiser as well as more economical to increase liability coverage to at least 100/300/25. The economy of this increase can be proved by the following graph.

REPRESENTATIVE LIABILITY COVERAGE RATES

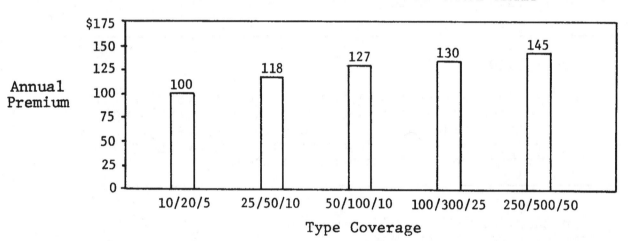

Model 1: How much more bodily injury coverage will one person receive by increasing the liability premium from $100 to $130 (an increase of 30%)?

At $100 premium the bodily injury coverage is $10,000 for one person. At $130 premium, the coverage increases to $100,000.

$$\text{Increase in coverage} = \frac{\$100,000 - \$10,000}{\$10,000}$$
$$= 900\%$$

12

Model 2: For an increase of $27 from the basic rate in premium, the insured can get an increase of $5,000 in property damage coverage. What are the comparative percentage changes?

$$\text{Percentage change in premium} = \frac{\$127 - \$100}{\$100}$$
$$= 27\%.$$

$$\text{Percentage change in coverage} = \frac{\$10,000 - \$5,000}{\$5,000}$$
$$= 100\%$$

Comprehensive insurance protects the policy holder from a great variety of unfortunate accidents that can occur while the car is not moving.

DEFINITION

Comprehensive coverage provides protection against fire, theft, acts of malice, vandalism, and acts of nature. In other words, it provides coverage for all damages that are not the result of an accident that occurs while the automobile is moving.

Medical-payments insurance pays for medical and burial expenses, regardless of who is at fault in an accident.

DEFINITION

Medical-payments coverage provides for the insured person and all passengers for medical costs that might result from an accident. The normal coverage is $2,000 for each person.

As with other forms of coverage, medical-payments premiums provide higher coverage at proportionally less cost.

TYPICAL MEDICAL PAYMENTS:
PREMIUM AND COVERAGE

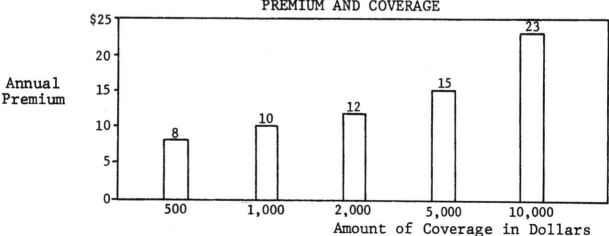

Model 1: What is the increase in dollars in the amount of payments covered by increasing the premium from $8 a year to $15 a year?

$15 premium coverage = $5,000
$ 8 premium coverage = - 500
Amount of increase   = $4,500

Model 2: The percentage increase in coverage made by increasing the premium rate from $8 to $12 (a 50% increase) turns out to be 300% ($500 to $2,000 for amount of coverage). What is the percentage increase made by increasing a $10 premium to a $15 premium (which is also a 50% increase)?

$$\text{Increase in coverage} = \frac{\$5,000 - \$1,000}{\$1,000} = 400\%$$

Another important category of insurance coverage is collision coverage, which applies regardless of who is to blame for the accident.

DEFINITION

Collision coverage provides protection for the owner's automobile against the risk of damages resulting from an accident. It is offered only with a deductible clause.

Most policies have a *deductible clause*, which means that the insured person is responsible for a stated amount (usually $50 or $100) of any loss that is covered that might occur. The insurance company pays the balance of the loss based on the market value of the car. The higher the deductible amount, the less cost to the insured person for collision coverage.

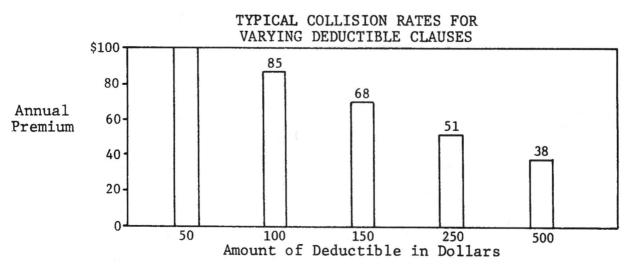

TYPICAL COLLISION RATES FOR VARYING DEDUCTIBLE CLAUSES

14

Model 1: What percentage increase in premium do you pay for collision coverage by decreasing the deductible clause from $500 to $100?

Premium for $500 deductible = $38
Premium for $100 deductible = $85

$$\text{Increase} = \frac{\$85 - \$38}{\$38} = 124\%$$

Model 2: You are considering changing from a $50-deductible collision coverage to a $250-deductible collision coverage. What are the comparative changes in premiums and deductibles?

$$\text{Change in premiums} = \frac{\$100 - \$51}{\$100} = 49\% \text{ less}$$

$$\text{Change in deductible coverages} = \frac{\$250 - \$50}{\$50}$$
$$= 400\% \text{ more}$$

The final category of coverage that will be discussed is the uninsured-motorist coverage. Approximately 15% of all drivers carry no insurance, which should give you an idea of the importance of carrying this kind of insurance.

DEFINITION

Uninsured-motorist coverage provides protection against three types of risk: (1) Motorists who are not insured, (2) hit and run accidents, and (3) accidents caused by drivers of stolen cars. The amount of coverage is usually $15,000 per person and $30,000 per accident.

Only eight states offer uninsured-motorist coverage for property damage as well as bodily injury. The maximum payout is limited by the individual state's financial responsibility law. Coverage limits normally vary from 10/20 to 25/50, or from $10,000 to $25,000 maximum paid for each person injured and from $20,000 to $50,000 for each accident's total injury liability. The premium rates usually run from $4 to $8 per year, which make this type of coverage a bargain.

Based on the previous tables, work the following insurance-coverage problems.

1.17   Type of coverage = liability
         Amount of coverage = 50/100/10
         Cost of annual premium?

_____

1.18   Type of coverage = liability
         Amount of coverage = 250/500/50
         Cost of annual premium?

_____

1.19   From your answers in Problems 1.17 and 1.18,
         what is the percentage increase in premiums?

_____

1.20   From your answers in Problems 1.17 and 1.18,
         what is the percentage increase in liability
         coverage for

         a. total bodily injury? _____

         b. property damage? _____

1.21   Type coverage = collision
         Amount of coverage = $50 deductible
         Cost of annual premium?

_____

1.22   Type coverage = collision
         Amount of coverage = $150 deductible
         Cost of annual premium?

_____

1.23   Based on your answers in Problems 1.21 and 1.22,
         what is the percentage decrease in premium payments?

_____

1.24   Based on your answers in Problems 1.21 and 1.22,
         what percentage increase occurs in the deductible
         amount?

_____

1.25   Type coverage = medical payments
         Amount of coverage = $5,000 per person
         Amount of premium?

_____

1.26   Type coverage = medical payments
        Amount of coverage = $1,000 per person
        Amount of premium?

        _____

1.27   Type coverage = medical payments
        Amount of coverage = $10,000 per person
        Amount of premium?

        _____

1.28   Based on your answers to Problems 1.25, 1.26, and
        1.27, how much does the premium increase in dollars
        from the lowest coverage to the highest coverage?

        _____

1.29   Based on your answer in Problem 1.28, what is the
        percentage increase

        a. in premiums?   _____

        b. in coverage?   _____

Review the material in this section in preparation for the Self Test. The Self
Test will check your mastery of this particular section. The items missed on this
Self Test will indicate specific areas where restudy is needed for mastery.

SELF TEST 1

Work the following interest-rate problems (each answer,
4 points).

1.01   Purchase price of car = $6,785
        Number of payments made in year = 12
        Number of payments made = 48
        Amount of monthly payment = $205
        True annual interest rate?

        _____

17

1.02   Purchase price of car = $4,500
        Amount of down payment = $450
        Number of payments made in year = 12
        Number of payments made = 28
        Amount of monthly payment = $165
        True annual interest rate?

        _____

1.03   Price of automobile = $6,800
        Amount of down payment = $700
        Number of payments made in year = 12
        Amount of monthly payment = $168
        True annual interest rate = 15.8%
        Number of payments?

        _____

1.04   Price of automobile = $11,500
        Down payment = $1,150
        Number of payments made in year = 12
        Number of payments made = 44
        True annual interest rate = 19.2%
        Amount of monthly payment?

        _____

Work the following automobile-operating cost problems (each
answer, 4 points).

1.05   Gas and oil costs = $1,000
        Miles driven = 10,000
        Cost per mile?

        _____

1.06   Gas and oil costs = $1,750
        Cost per mile = 9.5¢
        Miles driven?

        _____

1.07   Miles driven = 20,000
        Cost per mile = 11¢
        Gas and oil costs?

        _____

1.08   Cost of repairs = $550
        Cost of parts = $125
        Cost of maintenance = $120
        Miles driven = 14,000
        Cost per mile?

        _____

1.09   Cost of repairs = $150
        Cost of parts = $85
        Cost of maintenance = $125
        Cost per mile = 4.5¢
        Miles driven?

        _____

1.010   Cost of gas and oil = $1,950
        Cost of repairs, parts, and maintenance = $1,200
        Amount of depreciation = $900
        Annual insurance premium = $240
        Miles driven = 17,000
        Operating costs per mile?

        _____

1.011   Cost of gas and oil = $1,200
        Cost of repairs, parts, and maintenance = $1,000
        Amount of depreciation = $850
        Annual insurance premium = $250
        Miles driven = 18,000
        Operating costs per mile?

        _____

1.012   Purchase price of automobile = $4,500
        Market value of car = $1,850
        Years driven = 6
        Average miles driven per year = 15,000
        Cost of depreciation per mile?

        _____

1.013   Purchase price of automobile = $5,700
        Market value at resale = $3,700
        Years driven = 4
        Cost of depreciation per mile = 4¢
        Average miles driven per year?

        _____

1.014   Purchase price of automobile = $6,100
         Salvage value = $200
         Years driven = 10
         Average miles driven per year = 16,000
         Cost of depreciation per mile?

         _____

1.015   Purchase price of automobile = $3,995
         Years driven = 4
         Cost of depreciation per mile = 3¢
         Average miles driven per year = 14,125
         Market value at resale?

         _____

Work the following automobile-insurance problems (each answer, 4 points).

1.016   Policy A Costs $250 per year. Policy B costs $365
         per year. Policy A provides liability coverage of
         20/40/5. Policy B provides liability coverage of
         40/80/10. No other difference exists between the
         two policies. What is the percentage increase in
         premiums from policy A to policy B (policy B doubles
         the liability coverage of policy A)?

         _____

1.017   If Policy C provides a $50-deductible clause for
         collision insurance for $35, and a $100-deductible
         clause for collision insurance for $45, what is the
         percentage increase in premium rate for the $100
         deductible?

         _____

1.018   Two different policies giving the same coverage are
         shown in the following table. Which policy is
         less expensive?

Coverage	Policy A Premium	Policy B Premium
Liability 100/300/50	$135.00	$145.00
Comprehensive (actual cash value)	75.00	71.00
Collision ($100 deductible)	68.00	62.00
Medical payments ($2,500 per person)	17.50	14.50
Uninsured motorist ($12,500 per person and $25,000 per accident)	7.00	8.40

20

1.019　Based on your calculations in Problem 1.018, how much difference in annual premiums exists between policy *A* and policy *B*?

_____

II. TRANSPORTATION AND TRAVEL

OBJECTIVES

4. To work time, distance, and ratio problems.
5. To adjust time based on time zones.

Many times when you plan a trip, you wish to estimate your travel time so that you can inform others of your expected arrival time, or perhaps you want to know approximately what city you will arrive at for lunch. If you work for a travel agency, you need to know how to determine the times of travel, departure, and arrival at various destinations to plan someone's *itinerary* correctly.

TIME, DISTANCE, AND RATE

When you plan itineraries, you are concerned with time, distance, and rate calculations, and with time-zone adjustments. This section will give you practice in solving such problems.

PROCEDURE

To compute the distance covered, multiply the average speed by the time required to cover the distance. $d = rt$, where d is the distance covered in miles, r is the average rate of speed in miles per hour, and t is the time of travel in hours.

Note: Sometimes expressing distance in feet and rate of speed in seconds is more convenient than expressing the units in miles and miles per hour. To convert miles per hour to feet per second, multiply the speed given by $\frac{22}{15}$.

Model 1: You are planning a trip to the city. The distance is 270 miles. If you drive at an average speed of 45 mph and you leave at 1:30 p.m., what time should you arrive at the city limits?

$d = rt$; therefore, $t = \frac{d}{r}$

$t = \frac{270}{45} = 6$ hours

Therefore, time of arrival = 1:30 + 6 = 7:30 p.m.

Model 2: The train trip from Metropolis A to Metropolis B takes 4 hours and 15 minutes. If the rail distance between Metropolis A and Metropolis B is 250 miles, how fast must the train average?

4 hrs. 15 min. = 4.25 hrs.

$d = rt$ and $r = \dfrac{d}{t}$

$r = \dfrac{250}{4.25} = 58.82$ mph

Sometimes more than one automobile, train, or plane is involved in a problem. You may wish to know, for example, how far apart planes may be flying after flying a certain number of hours after leaving an airport at different time intervals. Or, perhaps, you want to know how many minutes one car will take to overtake another car, given each vehicle's time of departure and speed.

In any event, draw a diagram showing the respective rates, distances, and routes traveled by each vehicle to simplify the problem.

Model 3: Two trains leave the same station. Train 1 leaves at 4:30 p.m. and Train 2 leaves at 5:15 p.m. Both trains travel the same route, but Train 1 averages 56 mph, and Train 2, an express limited, averages 72 mph. The dispatcher needs to know if Train 1 can reach its destination, 126 miles away, ahead of Train 2, or if he must divert Train 2 onto another track to avoid a collision. Solve the problem.

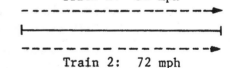

Train 1: $t = \dfrac{d}{r} = \dfrac{126}{56}$
$t = 2.25$ hr.

Therefore, Train 1 arrives at its destination at 4:30 + 2.25 hours, or 6:45 p.m.

Train 2: $t = \dfrac{d}{r} = \dfrac{126}{72}$
$t = 1.75$ hr.

Therefore, Train 2 arrives at its destination at 5:15 + 1.75 hours, or 7:00 p.m. Hence, Train 1 arrives at the destination 15 minutes ahead of Train 2 and with no danger.

Model 4:   Plane *A* leaves Albany at 2:25 p.m.,
averaging 350 mph and flying in a northerly
direction.   Plane *B* leaves Albany at 2:40 p.m.,
averaging 380 mph and flying due east.   At
5:25 p.m., how far apart will the planes be?

Plane *A*:
350 mph
Albany

distance apart
5:25 p.m.

Plane *B*:   380 mph

Plane *A*: $d = rt = 350(5{:}25 - 2{:}25) = 350(3)$
$= 1{,}050$ miles

Plane *B*: $d = rt = 380(5{:}25 - 2{:}40) = 380(2.75)$
$= 1{,}045$ miles.

From the diagram, we know that the respective
routes form a right triangle.   Also, we know
that in a right triangle the square of the
side opposite the right angle is equal to
the sum of the squares of the other two sides.

Side *A* was found to be 1,050 miles and
Side *B* was found to be 1,045 miles.

Therefore, $(\text{distance apart})^2 = 1{,}050^2 + 1{,}045^2$
$= 1{,}102{,}500 + 1{,}092{,}025$
$= 2{,}194{,}525$

Taking the square root of both sides of
the equation,

$\sqrt{(\text{distance apart})^2} = \sqrt{2{,}194{,}525}.$

Therefore, distance apart = 1,481.4 miles.

Model 5:   Two families are vacationing together,
driving in separate cars.   The Harris family
averages 45 mph, leaving Hometown 6 minutes
ahead of the Arlen family, who averages 58
mph.   How long will it take the Arlen family
to overtake the Harris family?

Both families are traveling the same
distance.   Therefore,
$d_H = d_A$, or $r_H t_H = r_A t_A$

Since the Harris family leaves 6 minutes before
the Arlen family, the former must drive $\frac{6}{60}$
hour longer than the Arlens.   So,

$45(t + \frac{6}{60}) = 58t$
$13t = 4.5$
$t = .346$ hr., or 20.8 minutes.

24

Work the following time, distance, and rate problems.

2.1   Average speed of automobile = 35 mph
       Time of travel = $2\frac{1}{2}$ hr.
       Distance traveled?

       _____

2.2   Distance between Town *A* and Town *B* = 420 miles
       Average speed of automobile = 45 mph
       Time to travel between Town *A* and Town *B*?

       _____

2.3   Distance between 2 airports = 1,505
       Average speed of airplane = 420 mph
       Flight time?

       _____

2.4   Distance between 2 airports = 2,400 miles
       Average speed of airplane = 450 mph
       Travel time by bus after arrival at airport = 35 minutes
       Total travel time?

       _____

2.5   Distance between Train 1 and Train 2 = 95 miles
       Average speed Train 1 = 45 mph
       Average speed Train 2 = 60 mph
       If both trains leave at the same time and travel
       toward each other but on parallel tracks, in how
       much time will their engines be opposite each other?
       (Hint: When the engines are opposite each other,
       together the trains will have traveled 95 miles.
       Their relative speed of travel is the sum of their
       respective speeds, or 105 mph.)

       _____

2.6   Average speed of Car 1 = 55 mph
       Average speed of Car 2 = 70 mph
       Time elapsed between start of Car 1
       and start of Car 2 = 4 minutes
       How long before Car 2 overtakes Car 1?

       _____

2.7   Speed of Plane *A* = 415 mph
             Speed of Plane *B* = 375 mph
             Both planes leave from New York City at same time
             Plane *A* flies due North
             Plane *B* flies due South
             After 4 hours, how far is Plane *A* from Plane *B*?

2.8   Two cars leave Phoenix and travel along roads
             90° apart. If Car 1 leaves 30 minutes earlier
             than Car 2 and averages 42 mph and if Car 2
             averages 50 mph, how far apart will they be
             after the car has traveled $3\frac{1}{2}$ hours?

TIME-ZONE ADJUSTMENTS

Often the traveler is confused when he makes adjustments in time based upon his travel across time zones. We have differences in time because of the earth's position relative to the sun. When the time is 5 p.m. in San Francisco, for example, it is 8 p.m. in New York and 1 a.m. the following day in London. If we did not have time zones, many places would be in daylight when the time was actually nighttime. To compensate for these differences in the sun's rising and setting throughout a standard 24-hour day, the world has adopted Greenwich (pronounced gren' ich) Time as the standard time from which all the world's clocks are adjusted based upon their relative distance from Greenwich, England.

DEFINITION

Greenwich Time is the standard time used in England and is the basis for setting standard time elsewhere. Standard time is reckoned by setting noon as the time the mean sun passes the prime meridian (the meridian passing through Greenwich). A *meridian* is a great circle that passes through any place on the earth's surface and through the North and South poles.

WORLD CITIES: STANDARD TIME DIFFERENCES

When it is 12 noon in New York (Easter Standard Time). The standard time in other cities is as follows:

City	Time	City	Time	City	Time	City	Time
Alexandria	7:00 P.M.	Damascus	7:00 P.M.	Lisbon	6:00 P.M.	Saigon	1:00 A.M.*
Amsterdam	6:00 P.M.	Delhi	10:30 P.M	London (Greenwich)	5:00 P.M.	Salt Lake City	10:00 A.M.
Anchorage	7:00 A.M.	Denver	10:00 A.M	Los Angeles	9:00 A.M.	San Francisco	9:00 A.M.
Athens	7:00 P.M.	Djakarta	12:00 MIDNIGHT	Madrid	6:00 P.M.	San Juan	1:00 P.M.
Auckland	5:00 A.M.*	Dublin	5:00 P.M.	Manila	1:00 A.M.*	Santiago	1:00 P.M.
Baghdad	8:00 P.M.	Fairbanks	7:00 A.M	Melbourne	3:00 A.M.*	Seattle	9:00 A.M.
Bangkok	12:00 MIDNIGHT	Frankfurt	6:00 P.M	Miami	12:00 NOON	Seoul	2:00 A.M.*
Barcelona	6:00 P.M.	Frobisher Bay	1:00 P.M	Monrovia	4:15 P.M.	Shanghai	1:00 A.M.*
Basra	8:00 P.M.	Gander	1:30 P.M	Montevideo	2:00 P.M.	Singapore	12:30 P.M.*
Beirut	7:00 P.M.	Geneva	6:00 P.M.	Moscow	8:00 P.M.	Stockholm	6:00 P.M.*
Berlin	6:00 P.M.	Glasgow	5:00 P.M	New Orleans	11:00 A.M.	Suva	5:00 A.M.*
Bogotá	12:00 NOON	Halifax	1:00 P.M	Nome	6:00 A.M.	Sydney	3:00 A.M.*
Bombay	10:30 P.M.	Hamilton (Bermuda)	1:00 P.M	Nouméa	4:00 A.M.	Tehran	8:30 P.M.
Boston	12:00 NOON	Havana	12:00 NOON	Oslo	6:00 P.M.	Tel Aviv	7:00 P.M.
Brussels	6:00 P.M.	Helsinki	7:00 P.M	Papeete (Tahiti)	7:00 A.M.	Tokyo	2:00 A.M.*
Bucharest	7:00 P.M.	Hong Kong	1:00 A.M.*	Paris	6:00 P.M.	Tucson	10:00 A.M.
Budapest	6:00 P.M.	Honolulu	7:00 A.M.	Peking	1:00 A.M.*	Valparaiso	1:00 P.M.
Buenos Aires	2:00 P.M.	Istanbul	7:00 P.M.	Phoenix	10:00 A.M.	Vancouver	9:00 A.M.
Cairo	7:00 P.M.	Jerusalem	7:00 P.M.	Portland	9:00 A.M.	Vienna	6:00 P.M.
Calcutta	10:30 P.M.	Johannesburg	7:00 P.M	Rangoon	11:30 P.M.	Vladivostok	2:00 A.M.*
Cape Town	7:00 P.M.	Juneau	9:00 A.M.	Recife	2:00 P.M.	Warsaw	6:00 P.M.
Caracas	1:00 P.M.	Karachi	10:00 P.M	Reykjavik	5:00 P.M.	Washington D.C.	12:00 NOON
Chicago	11:00 A.M.	Ketchikan	9:00 A.M	Rio de Janeiro	2:00 P.M.	Whitehorse	8:00 A.M.
Copenhagen	6:00 P.M.	Kinshasa	6:00 P.M	Rome	6:00 P.M.	Yokohama	2:00 A.M.*
Dakar	5:00 P.M.	Lima	12:00 NOON			Zürich	6:00 P.M.

* = FOLLOWING DAY

Model 1: A person is going to fly from New York to London. If he leaves at 4:00 p.m., Eastern Standard Time and the flight lasts 4½ hours, at what time should he set his watch when he arrives in London?

Since the flight lasts 4½ hours, the traveler must move his watch ahead to 4:00 p.m. + 4 hours, 30 minutes, or to 8:30 p.m. However, based on the time table provided, the time difference between New York and London is 5 hours. His watch should then be set at 8:30 p.m. + 5 hours, or at 1:30 a.m.

Model 2: You are flying from Phoenix to Tokyo. Your plane leaves Phoenix Tuesday evening at 6 p.m., Phoenix time. On what day and at what hour, Tokyo time, will you arrive in Tokyo assuming the flight takes 10 hours?

Since the flight takes 10 hours, move your watch ahead to 6 p.m. + 10 hours, or 4 a.m. The time difference between Phoenix and Tokyo is 16 hours (10:00 a.m. to 2:00 a.m. the following day). Add 16 hours to 4 a.m.; you will arrive in Tokyo at 8:00 p.m. on Wednesday night.

27

Most cities adopt *daylight-saving time* during the summer months to benefit from an additional hour of sunlight. The traveler needs to know how to adjust for time differences resulting from time-zone changes, and also changes resulting from daylight-saving time in some places.

DEFINITION

The Uniform Time Act of 1966 made the observance of *advanced (daylight) time* automatic throughout the country for the six-month period running from the last Sunday of April to the last Sunday of October. The only exceptions are the territories of Puerto Rico and the Virgin Islands and the states of Arizona, Hawaii, and the eastern half of Indiana.

Model 1:   You reside in Tucson, Arizona. On Sunday, April 27, daylight-saving time is to go into effect everywhere except for the places in the preceding definition. If your watch says the time is 7:00 a.m. in Tucson, what is the time in Los Angeles?

Normally, there is a one-hour time difference between Mountain and Pacific time zones; 7:00 a.m. in Tucson would be 6:00 a.m. in Los Angeles. However, because of daylight-saving time, people residing in Los Angeles will have to set their watches one hour ahead, which will make Los Angeles time and Tucson time the same. Thus, the time is 7:00 a.m. in Los Angeles also.

Model 2:   You are planning to drive from Flagstaff, Arizona, to Denver, Colorado, in August. You expect to leave at 8:00 a.m. on Tuesday, and stay overnight that night. You estimate the trip will take 24 hours. What time and what day do you expect to arrive in Denver?

Add 24 hours to 8:00 a.m., Tuesday, making the time 8:00 a.m. Wednesday. However, since Flagstaff is on Mountain Standard Time and Denver is on daylight-saving time, when it is 8:00 a.m. in Flagstaff, it is 9:00 a.m. in Denver. Therefore, you can expect to arrive in Denver at 9:00 a.m. on Wednesday.

Name _____

Date _____

Score _____

Consumer Mathematics 7 : LIFEPAC TEST

Compute the true annual interest rates for the following problems (each answer, 4 points).

1. $I = \dfrac{2(12)(360)}{2,400(24 + 1)}$

    $I = ?$

    _____

2. Price of automobile = $3,000
    Number of payments made in year = 12
    Number of payments made = 36
    Monthly payment amount = $93.33
    True annual interest rate?

    _____

3. Price of automobile = $5,555
    Down payment = $555
    Number of payments made in year = 12
    Number of payments made = 42
    True annual interest rate = 18%
    Monthly payment amount?

    _____

Work the following automobile-operating cost problems (each answer, 4 points).

4. Gas and oil costs = $1,000
    Parts, repairs, and maintenance costs = $800
    Operating cost per mile = 8.5¢
    Number of miles driven in year?

    _____

5. Cost of car = $3,800
    Years driven = 6
    Trade-in value = $1,250
    Average yearly depreciation?

    _____

6. Cost of car = $5,000
    Market value of car after first year = $3,800
    Cost of gas and oil = $750
    Cost of parts, repairs, and maintenance = $250
    Annual insurance premium = $300
    Miles driven in one year = 17,500
    Operating cost per mile driven?

    _____

Answer Questions 7 through 9 based upon the following insurance table (each answer, 4 points).

Coverage	Policy A Premium	Policy B Premium	Policy C Premium
Liability 100/200/50	$157	$152	$160
Comprehensive (actual cash value)	75	82	78
Collision ($100 deductible)	65	75	68
Medical payments ($5,000 per person)	22	30	20
Uninsured motorist ($15,000 per person and $30,000 per accident)	15	18	12

7.   What is the percentage of increase from the least expensive policy to the most expensive policy?

_____

8.   In terms of percentages, which policy has the lowest ratio of liability premium to total policy premium?

_____

9.   Considering liability, comprehensive, and collision coverages only, which policy is the most expensive?

_____

Work the following time, distance, and rate problems (each answer, 4 points).

10.   Distance covered by plane = 2,160 miles
Time required to cover distance = $4\frac{1}{2}$ hours
Average speed of airplane?

_____

11.   Car 1 leaves point A at 5:30 p.m., driving due south at an average speed of 35 mph. Car 2 leaves point A at 6:30 p.m., driving due north at an average speed of 45 mph. How far apart will the drivers be at 9:30 p.m.?

_____

12.   Train 1 leaves point A at noon traveling due west averaging 60 mph. Train 2 leaves point A at 1 p.m., traveling due north averaging 70 mph. How far apart will the trains be on a straight line distance at 4 p.m.?

_____

2

Calculate the following time-zone problems using the table,
"World Cities: Standard Time Differences" (each answer,
3 points).

13.   Month of year is August
         Time in Honolulu is 6:00 a.m.
         Time in Tucson?

         _____

14.   Standard time in Cairo is 4 p.m.
         Standard time in Peking?

         _____

Compute the following currency-exchange rates based on the
foreign-exchange table (each answer, 4 points).

15.   150 United States dollars
         How many Venezuelan bolivars based
         on the Tuesday quotation?

         _____

16.   1,500 Belgian francs
         How many United States dollars based
         on the Wednesday quotation?

         _____

Work the following foreign-exchange rate problems based on
the table "Foreign Exchange Rates: 1949-1977" (each answer,
4 points).

17.   How much has the Belgian franc appreciated compared to
         the United States dollar between 1949 and 1977, percentage-
         wise?

         _____

18.   Has the British pound appreciated or depreciated in
         value relative to the United States dollar over the
         years 1949 through 1977?

         _____

Work the following travel cost-benefit comparisons using the
appropriate charts (each answer, 4 points).

19.   What is the percentage increase in cost in going on a
         chartered airplane compared to going on a chartered
         ship based on a typical round-trip fare from New York
         to London?

         _____

20.   Compare travel in Spain and in Greece using the table
         shown previously for high and medium categories of daily
         tourist costs. What is the difference in dollars between
         the ranges of these two countries for the specified
         categories? (Note: one answer only.)

         _____

Questions 21 and 22 are based upon the Consumer Price Index figures shown in the following table. Use the figures under the heading "CPI-W" (each answer, 3 points).

Consumer Price Index by Cities

(1967 = 100, except Anchorage and Miami)

City[1]	1976 avg.	1977 (2)	February, 1978 CPI-U	CPI-W	March, 1978 CPI-U	CPI-W	April, 1978 CPI-U	CPI-W	May, 1978 CPI-U	CPI-W
Anchorage, Alas. (10/67 = 100)[3]	—	—	—	—	180.7	180.8	—	—	184.2	184.0
Atlanta, Ga.	169.2	184.5	186.1	186.5	—	—	188.5	188.9	—	—
Baltimore, Md.	173.9	190.7	—	—	—	—	—	—	198.0	198.4
Boston, Mass.	174.5	185.7(10)	—	—	188.2	187.8	—	—	190.7	190.2
Buffalo, N.Y.	170.6	185.1(11)	187.5	187.5	—	—	189.0	189.2	—	—
Chicago, Ill.-Northwest Ind.	165.1	180.0	184.2	183.8	186.3	185.6	187.3	186.6	188.0	188.2
Cincinnati, Ohio-Ky.-Ind.	170.1	186.7	—	—	—	—	—	—	197.5	197.6
Cleveland, Ohio	169.0	184.4(11)	186.6	186.6	—	—	190.3	190.7	—	—
Dallas-Ft. Worth, Tex.	167.7	183.8(11)	186.7	186.7	—	—	189.3	189.7	—	—
Denver-Boulder, Col.[3]	—	—	—	—	195.1	195.7	—	—	198.5	199.5
Detroit, Mich.	168.8	184.4	185.6	185.8	188.4	187.9	190.2	189.8	192.3	192.1
Honolulu, Ha.	162.8	174.9	178.0	177.5	—	—	181.4	181.3	—	—
Houston, Tex.	177.3	192.7(10)	—	—	—	—	—	—	—	—
Kansas City, Mo.-Kan.	166.5	182.7	183.8	184.4	—	—	186.9	186.6	—	—
Los Angeles-Long Beach, Anaheim, Cal.	168.0	184.4	186.5	186.8	187.4	187.1	189.6	186.9	191.5	191.2
Miami, Fla. (11/77 = 100)[3]	—	—	—	—	102.2	102.3	—	—	102.8	103.2
Milwaukee, Wis.	167.1	186.6(11)	—	—	186.3	186.5	—	—	188.7	189.5
Minneapolis-St. Paul, Minn.-Wis.	170.9	187.0(10)	—	—	—	—	—	—	—	—
New York, N.Y.-Northeast N.J.	176.3	186.8	190.8	190.8	192.2	191.9	193.5	192.6	194.6	193.7
Northeast Pa. (Scranton)	170.9	182.6(11)	—	—	187.0	187.2	—	—	190.0	190.8
Philadelphia, Pa.-N.J.	172.4	186.9	186.2	186.7	188.6	188.7	190.8	191.5	191.7	192.6
Pittsburgh, Pa.	168.3	183.5(10)	—	—	—	—	—	—	—	—
Portland, Ore.-Wash.	—	183.8	—	—	191.7	191.9	—	—	195.3	196.1
St. Louis, Mo.-Ill.	165.1	180.6	—	—	—	—	—	—	189.5	187.9
San Diego, Cal.	170.7	186.6	—	—	191.4	191.2	—	—	195.5	195.4
San Francisco-Oakland, Cal.	168.0	187.3	189.2	189.5	—	—	192.8	192.4	—	—
Seattle-Everett, Wash.	164.5	182.5(11)	—	—	187.2	186.8	—	—	193.5	192.5
Washington, D.C.-Md.-Va.	171.2	186.1(11)	—	—	191.5	191.4	—	—	194.7	196.7

(1) The area listed includes the entire Standard Metropolitan Statistical Area, except New York and Chicago which include the Standard Consolidated Area. (2) Latest month in 1977: usually Dec., except (10) = Oct. and (11) = Nov. (3) Anchorage, Denver and Miami are new additions to the special CPI city indexes.

21. For May, 1978, how much more, percentage-wise, was the cost of living in San Diego, California than the cost of living in Boston, Massachusetts?

_____

22. Using May, 1978, what was the range in index points in cost of living between the highest city and the lowest city?

_____

Answer the following customs-duty rate based on the customs duty chart (this answer, 4 points).

23. You buy two ski sweaters in Switzerland for $15 each. How much duty will you pay (disregard $100 deduction)?

_____

4

■ Work the following time-zone problems.

2.9   If the time is 6:00 p.m. in Chicago, what time
         is it in Jerusalem?

                                                                                 _____

2.10   Honolulu time = 12 noon
         Moscow time?

                                                                                  _____

2.11   Juneau, Alaska time = midnight
         Sydney time?

                                                                                  _____

2.12   Oslo time = 7:30 p.m.
         Flight time = 2 hours
         Warsaw arrival time?

                                                                                  _____

2.13   Rome time = 8:00 a.m.
         Flight time = 20 hours
         San Francisco arrival time?

                                                                                  _____

2.14   New York time = 4:00 p.m.
         Time of year = June
         Seattle time?

                                                                                   _____

2.15   Muncie (eastern Indiana) time = 12 noon
         Driving time = 16 hours
         Rest stop = 8 hours
         Time of year = July
         Arrival time at New York City?
         (Hint: Muncie is in the same time zone as
         New York City during standard time periods.)

                                                                                   _____

    Review the material in this section in preparation for the Self Test. This Self
Test will check your mastery of this particular section as well as your knowledge
of the previous section.

SELF TEST 2

The following problems are based on material covered in the
first part of the LIFEPAC. Work them according to the
requirements shown (each answer, 4 points).

2.01   Cost of car = $8,500
        Down payment = $850
        Number of payments in year = 12
        Number of payments made = 48
        Amount of monthly payment = $198
        True annual interest rate?

        _____

2.02   Cost of gas and oil = $780
        Cost of parts and repairs = $125
        Cost of servicing = $240
        Miles driven = 16,000
        Operating cost per mile?

        _____

2.03   Purchase price of car = $3,300
        Salvage value = $150
        Years driven = 10
        Average miles driven per year = 15,000
        Cost of depreciation per mile driven?

        _____

The following table shows two different policies. Answer
Questions 2.04 through 2.09 based on this data (each answer,
4 points).

Coverage	Policy A Premium	Policy B Premium
Liability 50/100/25	$125.00	$120.00
Comprehensive (actual cash value)	85.00	82.00
Collision ($100 deductible)	75.00	70.00
Medical payment ($2,500 per person)	15.50	19.50
Uninsured motorist ($15,000 per person; $30,000 per accident)	9.00	10.50

2.04   If the total premium is the only consideration, which
        policy appears to offer more coverage for the amount
        of money?

_____

2.05   What is the percentage difference between the two
        policies per year?

_____

2.06   If your only consideration between the two policies is
        the cost of insurance for medical payments and the
        cost of insurance for uninsured motorists, which policy
        will you buy?

_____

2.07   What is the difference in annual premiums between
        the two policies for the coverage described in
        Question 2.06?

_____

2.08   Does the difference calculated in Question 2.07 pay
        for the increased cost for liability coverage in
        Policy A?

_____

2.09   If your accident rate in the past has been one
        accident in 15 years, is paying the higher premium
        in Policy A for comprehensive insurance more
        sensible, economically, than paying the $100 -
        deductible for collision insurance in the same
        policy? Why?

_____

Work the following time, distance, and rate problems (each
answer, 4 points).

2.010   Average speed of train = 60 mph
        Time of travel = $2\frac{1}{4}$ hours
        Distance traveled?

_____

31

2.011   Distance between City *A* and City *B* = 259 miles
         Average speed of automobile = 37 mph
         Travel time?

         _____

2.012   Distance between City *X* and City *Y* = 231 miles
         Travel time = $5\frac{1}{2}$ hours
         Average speed of automobile?

         _____

2.013   Two trains leave from the same station at
         the same time but go in opposite directions.
         The first train averages 65 mph while the second
         train averages 57 mph. After they travel 7 hours,
         how far apart will they be?

         _____

2.014   Car *A* leaves Metrocenter at 1:00 p.m. going south
         and averaging 45 mph. Car *B* leaves Metrocenter at
         1:30 p.m. going west and averaging 55 mph. At
         2:00 p.m. how far apart will the two cars be in
         straight-line distance?

         _____

Work the following time zone-adjustment problems (each answer,
3 points).

2.015   If the standard time is 8 a.m. in London, what is
         the standard time in Cairo?

         _____

2.016   If the standard time is 12:00 midnight in Phoenix,
         what is the standard time in Juneau, Alaska?

         _____

2.017   City is Sydney
         Time is 6:30 p.m.
         Time in Honolulu?

         _____

2.018   Peking time is 8 a.m.
        New York time?

        _____

2.019   Phoenix time is 6 a.m. in July
        San Diego time?

        _____

57 / 71

Score _____

(✓) Teacher check _____
        Initial   Date

III. CURRENCY-EXCHANGE RATES AND TRAVEL-COST COMPARISONS

6. To calculate currency-exchange rates.
7. To make cost-benefit comparisons with regard to travel.

One of the challenges that face an international traveler is dealing in foreign currency. Rates of exchange between the United States dollar and another country's currency vary according to laws of supply and demand. Banks and other financial institutions go by the official rate of exchange. The unofficial rate promotes a degree of speculation and is not used by banks and other financial institutions.

The traveler can also save himself or herself a lot of unhappiness as well as expense if he or she is knowledgeable about certain practices in the travel business. These practices deal with travel cost-benefit comparisons.

We are not attempting to provide you with a complete list of "do's" and "don'ts", but rather are demonstrating with specific examples how you may benefit in your travels.

CURRENCY EXCHANGE RATES

To guard against unscrupulous dealers, you need to learn how to interpret foreign exchange quotations and to understand how to convert one currency to another currency when making transactions.

PROCEDURE

To convert United States dollars into a particular foreign currency, obtain the latest official foreign-exchange quotation. Two rates will be quoted: (1) Foreign currency into United States dollars and (2) United States dollars into foreign currency. If you want to convert United States dollars into foreign currency merely multiply the appropriate foreign-exchange currency figure by the number of United States dollars you wish or, conversely, if you wish to convert foreign currency into United States dollars, multiply the dollar-exchange rate by the amount of foreign currency you wish to exchange.

A typical two-day bank quotation of foreign-exchange rates is shown.

Model 1: You have $100 in United States bills. You wish to convert them to Argentine pesos. How many pesos will you obtain from the Wednesday quotation shown in the table at the right?

Since you are converting dollars to pesos, look at the Wednesday column headed "Dollar in foreign currency." On the left side find "Argentina." Where these two points meet, you should find the figure "900.50." Therefore, the number of pesos
= $100(900.50)
= 90,050 pesos.

Model 2: You go to a bank in Japan prior to leaving for the United States. You have 10,000 Japanese yen you wish to exchange for United States dollars. How many dollars will you get according to the Tuesday rate?

Look under the Tuesday column headed "Foreign currency in dollars." Find opposite Japan the figure ".005298." Since you will be going to the United States shortly, and you do not wish to speculate on the future official rate, ignore the figures opposite 30-, 60-, and 90-day future. Number of dollars = 10,000(.005298)
= $52.98

A table showing the average exchange rates for the years 1949 through March of 1977 is provided so that the student may gain some idea of how much fluctuation exists in foreign-exchange rates. Note that in the following table the foreign currencies are listed according to their conversion to United States cents, not to dollars.

Foreign exchange

NEW YORK (AP)—Foreign Exchange New York prices.

	Fgn. currency in dollars		Dollar in fgn. currency	
	Wed.	Tue.	Wed.	Tue.
Argentina	.0011	.0011	900.50	900.50
Australia	1.1485	1.1510	.8107	.8688
Austria	.0721	.0727	13.86	13.76
Belgium	.0337	.0339	29.64	29.52
Bolivia	.0520	.0520	19.20	19.20
Brazil	.0521	.0521	19.20	19.20
Britain	1.9660	1.9707	.5086	.5074
30 day fut.	1.9612	1.9672	.5098	.5083
60 day fut.	1.9591	1.9644	.5106	.5098
90 day fut.	1.9546	1.9617	.5116	.5097
Canada	.8486	.8520	1.1784	1.1737
30 day fut.	.8489	.8527	1.1779	1.1727
60 day fut.	.8499	.8536	1.1766	1.1715
90 day fut.	.8516	.8545	1.1742	1.1702
Chile	.0301	.0301	33.22	33.22
Colombia	.0250	.0250	40.04	40.04
Denmark	.1915	.1926	5.2230	5.1910
y Egypt	2.56	2.56	.3900	.3900
y Ecuador	.0371	.0371	26.95	26.95
France	.2301	.2312	4.3450	4.3250
Greece	.0274	.0274	36.45	36.45
Holland	.4878	.4911	2.0500	2.0360
Hong Kong	.2091	.2087	4.7830	4.7925
y India	.1290	.1290	7.7519	7.7519
Indonesia	.0024	.0024	415.00	415.00
Iran	.0142	.0142	70.45	70.45
x Israel	.0542	.0542	18.46	18.46
Italy	.00119	.001193	840.10	839.00
Japan	.00526	.005298	190.45	188.75
30 day fut.	.005297	.006376	188.78	186.00
60 day fut.	.005347	.005393	187.00	185.40
90 day fut.	.005387	.005433	185.60	184.05
Jordan	3.4106	3.4106	.2932	.2932
Kuwait	3.6744	3.6900	.2722	.2713
Lebanon	.3372	.3372	2.9650	2.9650
Mexico	.0439	.0439	22.79	22.79
New Zealand	1.0585	1.0600	.9447	.9433
Norway	.1990	.2004	5.0260	4.9000
y Peru	.0054	.0054	183.67	183.67
Philippines	.1358	.1358	7.3585	7.3585
Portugal	.0217	.0220	46.15	45.60
Saudi Arab	.3030	.3026	3.3000	3.3050
Singapore	.4578	.4593	2.1845	2.1770
So. Africa	1.1505	1.1507	.8691	.8620
Spain	.0141	.0141	71.00	70.85
Sweden	.2300	.2305	4.3460	4.3390
Switzerland	.6013	.6134	1.6465	1.6300
30 day fut.	.6122	.6190	1.6334	1.6155
60 day fut.	.6183	.6252	1.6173	1.5993
90 day fut.	.6252	.6319	1.5994	1.5825
Uruguay	.0148	.0148	6.7300	6.7300
Venezuela	.2329	.2329	4.2937	4.2937
W. Germany	.5257	.5294	1.9020	1.8887
30 day fut.	.5288	.5340	1.8910	1.8725
60 day fut.	.5325	.5377	1.8779	1.8596
90 day fut.	.5367	.5419	1.8632	1.8451

Midday prices at New York & San Francisco banks, gathered by Bank of America, New York. x—Floating.   y—Official rate.

FOREIGN EXCHANGE RATES: 1949-1977   SOURCE: Citibank (in U.S. cents)

Year	United Kingdom (pound)	Canada (dollar)	Netherlands (guilder)	West Germany* (deutsche mark)	Switzerland (franc)	France† (franc)	Belgium (franc)	Japan‡ (yen)	Italy (lira)
1949	368.72	92.88	34.53	N A	23.31	.3017	2.20	N A	.1699
1950	280.07	91.47	26.25	23.84	23.14	.2858	1.99	N A	.1601
1951	279.96	94.94	26.26	23.84	23.06	.2856	1.99	N A	.1600
1953	281.27	101.65	26.34	23.84	23.32	.2856	2.00	N A	.1600
1956	279.57	101.60	26.11	23.79	23.33	.2855	2.00	.2779	.1600
1958	280.98	103.03	26.42	23.85	23.33	.2858	2.00	.2779	.1601
1960	280.76	103.12	26.51	23.98	23.15	20.39	2.00	.2778	.1610
1962	280.78	93.56	27.76	25.01	23.12	20.41	2.01	.2771	.1611
1964	279.21	92.69	27.72	25.16	23.15	20.40	2.01	.2763	.1601
1966	279.30	92.81	27.63	25.01	23.11	20.35	2.01	.2760	.1601
1968	239.35	92.80	27.63	25.05	23.17	20.19	2.00	.2774	.1604
1970	239.59	95.80	27.65	27.42	23.20	18.09	2.01	.2792	.1595
1971	244.42	99.02	28.65	28.77	24.33	18.15	2.06	.2878	.1617
1972	250.08	100.94	31.15	31.36	26.19	19.83	2.27	.3300	.1713
1973	245.10	99.98	35.98	37.76	31.70	22.54	2.58	.3692	.1719
1974	234.03	102.26	37.27	38.72	33.69	20.81	2.57	.3430	.1537
1975	222.16	98.30	39.63	40.73	38.74	23.35	2.73	.3371	.1533
1976	180.48	101.41	37.85	39.74	40.01	20.94	2.59	.3374	.1204
1977 (March)	171.74	95.13	40.08	41.81	39.21	20.08	2.73	.3569	.1123

*Beginning with June 1950. † Beginning with 1960, 100 old francs = 1 new franc. ‡ Beginning with November 1956. N A = Not available.

Model 1: Between the years 1966 and 1976 how much has the United Kingdom pound changed relative to the United States dollar?

Look under the column headed "United Kingdom." Opposite the year 1966 note the figure 279.30. This figure means that in 1966, 1 United Kingdom pound could be exchanged for 279.30 United States cents, or $2.79. Opposite 1976 note the figure 180.48. One United Kingdom pound equaled $1.805, rounded off. The United Kingdom pound declined in value, therefore, by this percentage:

$$\text{Decline in United Kingdom pound} = \frac{\$2.793 - \$1.805}{\$2.793}$$
$$= .354, \text{ or } 35.4\%.$$

Model 2: Sometimes the United States dollar declines relative to certain other currencies such as the German deutsch mark and the Japanese yen. From 1956 to March 1977, how much has the American dollar declined relative to both the mark and the yen?

Year	Deutsche Mark	Yen
1956	23.79	.2779
1977	41.81	.3569

$$\text{Decline relative to mark} = \frac{41.81 - 23.79}{23.79}$$
$$= 75.8\%$$

$$\text{Decline relative to yen} = \frac{.3569 - .2779}{.2779}$$
$$= 28.4\%.$$

36

███████ Work the following foreign-exchange problems using the
tables previously provided.

3.1   Currency on hand = 5,000 Mexican pesos
         Currency desired = United States dollars
         How many United States dollars based on
           Wednesday quotation?

_____

3.2   Currency on hand = $100 United States dollars
         Currency desired = Israeli pounds
         How many pounds based on Tuesday rate?

_____

3.3   Currency on hand = 2,000 Swiss francs
         Currency desired = Dutch guilders (Holland)
         How many guilders based on Wednesday rate?
         (Hint: Convert 2,000 Swiss francs to United States
         dollars. Then convert United States dollars into
         guilders.)

_____

3.4   Currency on hand = 100,000 Brazilian cruzeiros
         Currency desired = United States dollars
         How many dollars based on Wednesday rate?

_____

3.5   Between the years 1970 and 1976, what percentage
         change in the rate of exchange occurred in the
         Swiss franc relative to the United States dollar?

_____

3.6   Based on your calculations in Problem 3.5, has
         the Swiss franc depreciated or *appreciated*?

_____

3.7   How much has the Canadian dollar relative to the
         United States dollar changed (as a percentage) from the
         years 1956 through 1976?

_____

3.8   Based on your calculations in Problem 3.7, has
         the Canadian dollar appreciated or depreciated
         during the stated period?

_____

First, we shall examine the mode of travel.
If the speed of travel is your main
consideration, the airlines offer the best
mode of transportation. Rates are very
competitive, and you can usually get
attractive discounts by arranging your air
travel through a reputable travel agency
that offers group-package tours. The
following fare comparisons for international
travel are based upon several air fares and
ship fares. Even though the data presented
are not current, they do provide a realistic
basis for comparisons.

Air Fares and Ship Fares

Type Travel	Sample Round-Trip Fares from New York to London
First-Class Air Fare	$754.30
First-Class Ship Fare	775.20
Regular Economy Air Fare	440.80
Tourist Class Ship Fare	408.00
Peak Season Economy Air Fare	526.30
Peak Season Tourist Class Ship Fare	470.25
14- to 21-Day Excursion Air Fare	331.00
30-Day Excursion Ship Fare	345.95
Charter Group (25 Persons or More) Air Fare	331.00
Charter Group (25 Persons or More) Ship Fare	306.00

Model 1: How much more does a round-trip ticket
from New York to London cost if you go
first-class by ship rather than first-
class by air?

First-class ship fare = $775.20
First-class air fare = 754.30
                        $ 20.90

What percentage savings is this?

Percentage savings = $\frac{\$20.90}{\$775.20}$ = 2.7%

Model 2: Considering only comparable fare classifications, which classification offers the greatest percentage difference between air travel and ship travel?

Regular economy air fare = $440.80
Tourist class ship fare = 408.00
                            $ 32.80; $\frac{\$32.80}{\$440.80} = 7.4\%$

Peak season economy air fare = $526.30
Peak season tourist ship fare = 470.25
                                 $ 56.05; $\frac{\$56.05}{\$526.30}$
                                        = 10.6\%

14- to 21-day excursion air fare = $331.00
30-day excursion ship fare   = 345.95
                                    $ 14.95;

                                    $\frac{\$14.95}{\$345.95} = 4.3\%$

Charter group air fare = $331.00
Charter group ship fare = 306.00
                           $ 25.00; $\frac{\$25.00}{\$331.00} = 7.6\%$

Therefore, the Peak-season classification offers the greatest percentage difference at 10.6%.

The question of safety often arises concerning flying. The International Civil Aviation Organization has been maintaining safety records of the world scheduled airlines since 1950. The following table lists the numbers of accidents and people killed as a result of air crashes.

SAFETY RECORD: WORLD SCHEDULED AIRLINES[1]
SOURCE: International Civil Aviation Organization

Year	Number of Accidents: Passenger-carrying Aircraft	Number of Passengers Killed	Fatality Rate (per 100 million Pass.-Mi.)	Fatal Accidents (per 100 million Mi. Flown)	Fatal Accidents [†]	Year	Number of Accidents: Passenger-carrying Aircraft	Number of Passengers Killed	Fatality Rate (per 100 million Pass.-Mi.)	Fatal Accidents (per 100 million Mi. Flown)	Fatal Accidents [†]
1950	27	551	3.15	3.02	0.54	1967	30	678	0.40	0.91	0.29
1952	21	386	1.54	1.90	0.34	1968	35	912	0.47	0.91	0.32
1954	28	443	1.36	2.19	0.42	1969	32	946	0.43	0.77	0.27
1956	27	552	1.25	1.71	0.34	1970	28	687	0.29	0.64	0.23
1958	30	609	1.15	1.65	0.34	1971	31	867	0.34	0.71	0.25
1960	34	873	1.29	1.71	0.38	1972	42	1,210	0.42	0.94	0.34
1962	29	778	1.97	1.44	0.37	1973	36	862	0.27	0.77	0.28
1964	25	616	0.58	1.09	0.30	1974	29	1,301	0.38	0.63	0.23
1965	25	684	0.56	0.98	0.29	1975	19	441	0.12	0.41	0.15
1966	31	1,001	0.70	1.12	0.33	1976	20	726	0.19	0.42	0.15

[†] Per 100.00 aircraft hours. [1] Excluding U.S.S.R. and China.

Model 1:   What was the percentage increase or decrease
in fatality rates between 1950 and 1975?

Look at the column headed "Fatality Rate
(per 100 million Passenger-Miles)." Note
figure "3.15" opposite 1950 and the figure
"0.12" opposite 1975. Since the rate has
decreased, calculate the percentage of
decrease:

$$\text{Percentage decrease in fatality rate} = \frac{3.15 - 0.12}{3.15}$$
$$= 96.2\%$$

Model 2:   What was the percentage increase or
decrease in fatal accidents ratios
between 1960 and 1970?

Look at the column headed "Fatal Accidents,"
which is the ratio of such accidents per
100,000 aircraft hours.

1960 fatal accident rate = 0.38
1970 fatal accident rate = 0.23

Since the rate has gone down, calculate
the percentage of decrease:

$$\text{Percentage decrease in fatal accident rate} = \frac{0.38 - 0.23}{0.38}$$
$$= 39.5\%$$

Accommodations, food, tours, and
gratuities are important items for the
traveler's budget. Since prices are
subject to change, the following figures
should not be considered as precise
amounts; but they should be viewed as
representative of the variance between
types of accommodations in different
places. The following table is a typical
list of prices by general category for
several continents.

Average Daily Cost for an American Tourist

	Europe	Far East and Pacific	South America
Lodging	$7.50-8.50	$7.50-8.50	$10.00-11.00
Food	6.20-7.75	6.00	9.00
Other Expenses (Including Transportation, Admissions, and Miscellaneous)	7.00-8.75	7.50	10.00
Totals	$20.70-25.00	$21.00-22.00	$29.00-30.00

Model 1: Which trip will cost you more: 30 days in South America or 40 days in the Far East?

Use the high average daily totals for South America and for the Far East and multiply each by their respective days.

South American expense = 30($30) = $900
Far Eastern expense = 40($22) = $880

Therefore, from the data given, 30 days in South America will cost you slightly more than 40 days in the Far East.

Model 2: With respect to food, which region has the least expensive average daily food expense? What is the percentage increase between the lowest average and the highest average as shown in the preceding table?

The least expensive region is the Far East at $6.00 per day.

The most expensive region is South America at $9.00 per day.

The percentage increase = $\dfrac{\$9 - \$6}{\$6}$ = 0.5, or 50%

Quite naturally, the variances among countries are considerable. The following table lists some countries with their respective high category of average costs per day and medium category of average costs per day. Each category's expenses

41

include the daily costs of hotel plus
meals, porters, theaters, tips, two trips
in a local city bus, and expenditures for
such things as clothes pressing, newspapers,
and so on.

Average Costs per Day

Country	High Category	Medium Category
Argentina	$22.55	$10.80
Austria	17.08	10.17
Belgium	20.16	12.96
Brazil	18.33	12.25
England	22.94	15.88
France	29.04	19.54
Greece	16.55	9.48
Italy	21.84	14.69
Netherlands	20.80	14.37
Spain	14.51	8.79
Sweden	23.51	15.73
Switzerland	21.57	13.82
United States	34.48	22.46
West Germany	22.53	14.33
Yugoslavia	10.96	7.38

Model 1: Considering the high category only, what
is the percentage increase between daily
expenses in Greece and Italy?

Italy = $21.84
Greece = $16.55

Percentage increase = $\dfrac{\$21.84 - \$16.55}{\$16.55}$ = 32% more

expensive in Italy.

Model 2: Considering the medium category only, what is the percentage increase. between the cost in the country with the lowest cost and the cost in the country with the highest cost?

Highest cost is United States at $22.46. Lowest cost is Yugoslavia at $7.38.

Difference is $22.46 - $7.38 = $15.08.

Percentage increase is $\frac{\$15.08}{\$7.38}$ = 2.04.

Therefore, the cost increase is a little more than twice (204%) as much in the United States as it is in Yugoslavia.

Few American travelers take advantage of the many cost savings available to the prudent individual. Travel abroad, especially, can be a very expensive luxury to the unsuspecting person. Some of the savings in transportation costs have been briefly explored previously. However, other savings exist also. For example, when traveling in Europe, the bargain seeker can purchase such passes as the Eurailpass, the Eurotoupass, and the Eurotelpass. Buying these passes is like having money in the bank. For $130, one can purchase a month's Eurailpass that permits unlimited use of trains in 13 countries on the continent. This pass is much more economical than a round-trip first-class ticket from Paris to Rome for $77.65.

When ordering beverages, stick to the local products. Not only are they generally of good quality, but they can save the buyer up to two-thirds of the cost of imported beverages.

With respect to tipping, you are wise to tip in the local currency, since you will generally overtip if you use United States currency. A good rule of thumb is to tip between 15% and 20% of your bill.

Taxis are expensive, so try to learn the schedules and routes of buses, subways, and local trains.

If you are purchasing merchandise abroad to bring back to the United States, check the customs duties. Every resident of the United States who has been out of the country for at least 48 hours is entitled to one hundred dollars' worth of articles duty-free. Also, articles valued at $10 or less are free of duty. The following table provides the basis for determining how much duty one must pay for selected articles based on their value or acquisition cost.

Article	Duty Levied in Per Cent of Its Cost
Automobiles, new and used	$6\frac{1}{2}$
Cameras	15
Chinaware	35
Dresses	21
Jewelry, gold, platinum, or silver	24
Lace, shawls, and scarves	$42\frac{1}{2}$
Luggage and handbags	20
Pearls, strung	55
Shirts	25
Sweaters, including Cashmere	20
Toys, mechanical	44
Watches, 18 jewels and over	$10.75

Model 1: You purchase a Cashmere sweater in London for $35. When you return to the United States, how much duty will you pay? (Assume you have used your duty-free exemption.)
Duty rate of Cashmere sweater = 20%
Amount of duty = $35(0.20) = $7.00.

Model 2: You purchase the following articles abroad; a camera for $135; mechanical toys for $50; strung pearls for $75; and a lace shawl for $8.50. If you have not used your duty-free exemption, how much will you pay for the articles?

Take the most expensive article, the camera, and apply the $100 exemption. The amount of $35 remains to be figured at the prevailing duty rate.

```
Cost of camera to you = $135 + $35(0.15) = $140.25
Cost of toys to you = $50 + $50(0.44) =     72.00
Cost of pearls to you = $75 + $75(0.55) =   116.25
Cost shawl to you = $8.50 + $0 =             8.50
                                           _____
        Total cost of all articles =      $337.00
```

███ Work the following travel problems based on the data provided in the various tables in this section.

3.9   How much less money does a round-trip plane ticket from New York to London cost one who goes with a charter group rather than a regular economy class?

_____

3.10 What percentage increase occurs in the price of a round-trip plane ticket from New York to London by electing to go during the peak season as opposed to going on the economy class?

_____

3.11 What percentage savings does a person obtain on a round-trip ticket from New York to London if he chooses to go tourist class on a ship as opposed to going first class on a ship?

_____

3.12 With respect to air safety, in which year between 1950 and 1976 did the majority of air fatalities occur, and how many passengers were killed in that year?

_____

3.13 What percentage decrease occurred in air fatalities between the "high year" and the following year?

_____

The following table indicates certain airline traffic volume data. Answer Questions 3.14 through 3.16 based on this table.

AIRLINE TRAFFIC VOLUME SOURCE: International Civil Aviation Organization

According to estimates released in March 1977 by the International Civil Aviation Organization for its 135 member states, in 1976 the airlines carried 473 million passengers for a total of 632,000 million passenger kilometers (393,000 million passenger miles) on scheduled services, representing increases of 10 per cent over 1975.

Year	Miles Flown	Hours Flown	Passengers Carried	Passenger-Miles	Average Number of		
					Passengers per Aircraft	Miles Flown per Passenger	Miles Flown per hr.
	(In Millions)						
1976	4,800	12.9	473	393,000	82	831	372
1975	4,670	12.6	436	356,000	76	817	371
1974	4,580	12.5	424	340,000	74	802	366
1973	4,660	12.7	405	323,000	69	798	357
1972	4,480	12.2	368	288,500	64	784	357
1971	4,390	12.2	333	253,500	58	771	360
1970	4,355	12.1	311	237,500	55	762	360
1969	4,170	11.8	293	218,000	52	744	354
1968	3,730	11.0	262	192,500	52	736	339
1967	3,290	10.2	233	169,500	52	727	320
1966	2,790	9.3	200	142,000	51	711	301

3.14   Between 1966 and 1976 by what percentage did the average number of passengers per aircraft increase?

_____

3.15   What was the percentage increase in average miles flown per hour over the years listed?

_____

3.16   Is the statement true that between 1966 and 1976 the average number of miles flown per passenger increased by one-third?

_____

For the following questions use the tables and charts shown in this section.

3.17   The range of typical total prices for an American tourist traveling on the European continent is $20.70 to $25.00. What is the average price?

_____

3.18   Based on your answer in Question 3.17, is the average price higher or lower than the highest total figure shown for the Far East and Pacific area?

_____

3.19   According to the table listing average daily
        expenses for a tourist by country based on high
        and medium categories, Brazil has a range from
        $12.25 to $18.33, and Greece has a range from $9.48
        to $16.55. Which of the two countries has the larger
        range in categories?

        _____

3.20   By what percentages are Sweden's high category and
        medium category less than the United States' categories?
        (Note: Two answers are necessary.)

        _____

        _____

3.21   For the conditions shown, could the general statement
        be said that the typical tourist pays about twice as
        much per day to reside in West Germany as he would pay
        in Yugoslavia?

        _____

3.22   A United States citizen returning to the States
        declares the following items at the customs office:

        4 shirts at $8.50 each
        3 dresses at $27.50 each
        1 pair of gold cuff links at $17.50 per pair

        How much duty should he pay?   _____

3.23   Another United States traveler arrives at a United
        States point of entry. He has purchased a Fiat car
        abroad that cost him $4,250. How much duty does he
        have to pay?

        _____

3.24   Based on your answer in Question 3.23, what would be the
        total cost to the traveler for the Fiat?

        _____

3.25   You are returning to the United States from a trip to
        Latin America. You purchased the following items:

        4 lace shawls at $25 each
        gold jewelry for $150
        chinaware for $215

        How much duty must you pay?   _____

3.26   Based on your answer in Question 3.25, what percentage
        of the cost of these articles do you pay in duty?

        _____

3.27   If you later find that you could have gotten the same
        goods in the United States for a 30% markup; would
        you have saved more by buying them in the United
        States than in Latin America (ignoring cost of travel)?

        _____

 Before you take this last Self Test, you may want to do one or more of
these self checks.

1. ____ Read the objectives. Determine if you can do them.

2. ____ Restudy the material related to any objectives that you cannot do.

3. ____ Use the SQ3R study procedure to review the material:

   a. **S**can the sections,
   b. **Q**uestion yourself again (review the questions you wrote
      initially),
   c. **R**ead to answer your questions,
   d. **R**ecite the answers to yourself, and
   e. **R**eview areas you didn't understand.

4. ____ Review all activities, and Self Tests, writing a correct answer for
        each wrong answer.

SELF TEST 3

Work the following interest-rate problems (each answer, 4 points).

3.01   Purchase price of car = $3,500
        Allowance for trade = $500
        Number of payments in year = 12
        Number of payments made = 24
        Amount of monthly payment = $147.50
        True annual interest rate?

        _____

3.02   Purchase price of car = $2,850
        Trade-in value = $1,750
        Years driven = 3
        Cost of depreciation per mile driven = 4¢
        Average number of miles driven per year?

        _____

3.03   Price of automobile = $5,250
        Number of payments made in year = 12
        Number of payments made = 36
        Amount of monthly payment = $185
        True annual interest rate?

        _____

Work the following automobile operating costs problems (each answer, 4 points).

3.04   Cost of gas and oil = $850
        Cost of parts and repairs = $200
        Miles driven = 18,000
        Operating cost per mile = 9¢
        Cost of servicing?

        _____

3.05   Cost of car = $4,000
        Years driven = 3
        Trade-in value = $2,500
        Average yearly depreciation?

        _____

3.06   Cost of car = $4,500
        Market value of car after first year = $3,500
        Cost of gas and oil = $550
        Cost of parts, repairs, and maintenance = $275
        Annual insurance premium = $700
        Miles driven in one year = 15,000
        Operating cost per mile driven?

        _____

Work the following automobile-insurance problems based on the given insurance table (each answer, 4 points).

	Policy A Premium	Policy B Premium
Liability 100/300/25	$130	$138
Comprehensive (actual cash value)	72	75
Collision ($100 deductible)	65	67
Medical payments ($2,000 per person)	18	14
Uninsured motorist ($15,000 per person and $30,000 per accident)	12	10

3.07　　If you are most interested in the costs for comprehensive insurance and for collision insurance, which policy will you buy?

_____

3.08　　What is the percentage decrease in cost from Policy A's medical insurance to Policy B's medical insurance?

_____

Work the following time, distance, and rate problems (each answer, 4 points).

3.09　　Distance between City P and City Q = 345 miles
　　　　Time required to cover distance = 7.5 hours
　　　　Average speed of car?

_____

3.010　　Plane 1 leaves Kennedy Airport at 6:00 p.m. and flies on a heading of 165° averaging 400 mph. Plane 2 leaves Kennedy Airport at 6:30 p.m. and flies on the same heading averaging 425 mph. At what time will Plane 2 overtake Plane 1?

_____

3.011　Car *A* travels north from point *D* at 3 p.m. averaging 55 mph. Car *B* travels east from point *D* at 4 p.m. averaging 50 mph. How far apart will the cars be on a straight-line distance at 4:30 p.m.?

_____

Work the following time zone-adjustment problems (each answer, 3 points).

3.012　Month of year is July
　　　　Time in Phoenix is 8:00 a.m.
　　　　Time in New York?

_____

3.013　Standard time in Warsaw is 6 p.m.
　　　　Standard time in London?

_____

Work the following currency-exchange problems (each answer, 4 points).

3.014　Based on the foreign-exchange table, convert 15,000 Italian lira into United States dollars (Wednesday rate).

_____

3.015　Convert $500 in United States currency to Venezuelan bolivars, using Tuesday's exchange rate.

_____

3.016　Convert 1,200 Chilean escudos into United States dollars, based on Wednesday's exchange rate.

_____

Problems 3.017 through 3.019 are based upon the following table. Work the money-depreciation rates as required (each answer, 4 points).

MONEY DEPRECIATION: ANNUAL RATES   Source: Citibank
The value of money is here measured by reciprocals of official cost-of-living or consumer price indexes.

	INDEXES: VALUE OF MONEY			RATE OF DEPRECI- ATION		INDEXES: VALUE OF MONEY			RATE OF DEPRECI- ATION		INDEXES: VALUE OF MONEY			RATE OF DEPRECI- ATION
	1965	1970	1975	1970-75		1965	1970	1975	1970-75		1965	1970	1975	1970-75
Venezuela	100	92	70	5.4	Denmark	100	73	47	8.5	Greece	100	88	49	11.0
West Germany	100	88	65	5.8	South Africa	100	85	55	8.5	Peru	100	63	35	11.2
Honduras	100	92	68	5.9	Iran	100	93	59	8.6	United Kingdom	100	80	43	11.5
United States	100	81	59	6.3	Singapore	100	94	57	9.1	Trinidad/Tobago	100	83	45	11.6
Luxembourg	100	86	61	6.7	Australia	100	86	53	9.3	Ireland	100	77	41	11.7
Panama	100	92	65	6.7	New Zealand	100	79	48	9.3	Jamaica	100	77	39	12.9
Austria	100	85	60	6.8	Kenya	100	91	54	9.9	Portugal	100	74	36	13.1
Canada	100	83	58	6.8	Ecuador	100	79	42	10.2	S. Korea	100	53	29	13.1
Malaysia	100	94	66	6.8	Italy	100	86	55	10.2	Philippines	100	75	37	13.2
Switzerland	100	85	58	7.1	Japan	100	77	45	10.2	Turkey	100	67	29	15.7
Sweden	100	80	55	7.3	Paraguay	100	94	54	10.3	Zaire	100	35	15	15.7
Belgium	100	84	56	7.7	Finland	100	64	37	10.4	Bolivia	100	75	32	15.8
Norway	100	79	53	7.7	India	100	72	42	10.4	Colombia	100	62	26	16.0
Netherlands	100	79	52	7.9	Mexico	100	84	47	10.8	Yugoslavia	100	59	24	16.1
Thailand	100	88	58	8.0	Spain	100	78	44	10.8	Israel	100	82	32	17.3
France	100	81	53	8.1	China (Taiwan)	100	81	45	10.9	Brazil	100	30	11	17.4
										Argentina	100	41	*	39.2
*Less than 1.										Chile	100	31	*	67.5

3.017   Among the countries of Peru, Trinidad/Tobago, Jamaica, Bolivia, Colombia, Brazil, Argentina, and Chile, what was their average rate of depreciation over the period given?

_____

3.018   For the period 1970 through 1975 the table shows the average United States rate of money depreciation as 6.3%. How much more or less does this rate differ from the average rate shown for France?

_____

3.019   West Germany has one of the smallest rates of money depreciation for the period given. How much better percentage-wise was West Germany's rate of money depreciation compared to Japan's rate of money depreciation?

_____

52

Work the following travel cost-benefit problems (each answer, 4 points).

3.020   According to the table on the safety record of the world scheduled airlines, the number of fatal accidents per 100,000 aircraft hours has been declining since 1950. What was the percentage rate of decline from 1950 to 1976?

_____

3.021   From the round-trip air fare and ship fare table, how much would a traveler save percentage-wise by taking the 14- to 21-day excursion air fare than by going on the regular economy air fare?

_____

3.022   Refer to the table of average costs per day by country provided previously. What is the range between the high category and the medium category for the Netherlands?

_____

3.023   To live expensively in West Germany, how much more does the tourist pay than if he lives moderately in Italy?

_____

Answer the following customs duty-rate problems (each answer, 4 points).

3.024   How much more is the duty levied on chinaware that costs a traveler $125 (without subtracting the $100 worth of duty-free articles) than the duty levied on an 18-jewel watch?

_____

3.025   If you buy a Mercedes-Benz car for $15,000 in Germany, how much duty will you have to pay when you ship it back to the United States?

_____

Answer the following questions based on the airline traffic-volume table (each answer, 4 points).

3.026   From the airline traffic-volume table, how much
         faster did airlines average in miles flown per hour
         between 1970 and 1976?

         _____

3.027   Between 1966 and 1974, how many more passengers on the
         average were carried per aircraft?

         _____

Score   _____
Teacher check _____
               Initial   Date

REVIEW   Before taking the LIFEPAC Test, you may want to do one or more of these self
          checks.

    1. _____ Read the objectives. Check to see if you can do them.
    2. _____ Restudy the material related to any objective that you cannot do.
    3. _____ Use the SQ3R study procedure to review the material.
    4. _____ Review activities, Self Tests, and LIFEPAC Glossary.
    5. _____ Restudy areas of weakness indicated by the last Self Test.

GLOSSARY

appreciated. To have risen in value.

bodily injury insurance. Offers protection covering injury to other passengers during an accident involving the policy-holder's vehicle.

collision coverage. Provides protection for the owner's automobile against the risk of damages resulting from an accident, and is offered only with a deductible clause.

comprehensive coverage. Provides protection against fire, theft, acts of malice, vandalism, and acts of nature.

daylight-saving time. Time that is one hour advanced of standard time and is in effect for the six-month period extending from the last Sunday of April to the last Sunday of October.

depreciation. A lessening or lowering in value.

gratuities. Presents of money in return for services; tips.

Greenwich Time. The standard time used in England and is the basis for setting time elsewhere.

itinerary. A route or plan of travel.

liability. The state of being responsible. A person at fault in an accident is said to be liable for the accident. Liability insurance is the protection of the one who is liable from suits by others.

medical payments coverage. Provides protection for the insured person and all passengers for medical costs that might result from an accident.

meridian. A great circle that passes through any place on the earth's surface and through the North and South poles.

property damage insurance. Offers protection against losses incurred to property belonging to persons other than the policy holder.

uninsured-motorist coverage. Provides protection against motorists who are not insured, against hit-and-run accidents, and against accidents caused by drivers of stolen cars.